Can You Carry?

By Kathy Bartlett

Linda Henderson & Holly Gibbons

Copyright © 2015 Porch Music Store

All rights reserved.

ISBN-13:
978-1519174840

ISBN-10:
1519174845

DEDICATION

This book is dedicated to the child within all of us.
May music keep your inner child filled with joy.

CONTENTS

Acknowledgments — Pg 9

1. How to Play — Pg 11
2. Canjo String Replacement — Pg 13
3. Alouetta — Pg 15
4. Alphabet Song — Pg 16
5. Baa Baa Black Sheep — Pg 17
6. Bingo — Pg 18
7. Buffalo Girls — Pg 19
8. Camptown Races — Pg 20
9. Clementine — Pg 21
10. Farmer in the Dell — Pg 22
11. Frere Jacque — Pg 23
12. Go Tell Aunt Rhodie — Pg 24
13. Happy Birthday — Pg 25
14. Home on the Range — Pg 26
15. Hot Cross Buns — Pg 27
16. Hush Little Baby — Pg 28
17. I Love You — Pg 29
18. Little Teapot — Pg 30
19. Itsy Bitsy Spider — Pg 31
20. It's Raining… — Pg 32
21. Jesus Loves Me — Pg 33
22. Kumbayah — Pg 34
23. London Bridge — Pg 35
24. Mary Had a Little Lamb — Pg 36
25. Oh Suzanna — Pg 38
26. Old McDonald — Pg 39
27. On Top of Old Smokey — Pg 40
28. Pop Goes the Weasel — Pg 41
29. Pussy Cat — Pg 42
30. Red River Valley — Pg 43
31. Row, Row, Row Your Boat — Pg 44
32. Short'nin' Bread — Pg 45
33. Skip to my Lou — Pg 46
34. Sleep Little Baby — Pg 47

CONTENTS
Cont.

35	Ten Little Indians	Pg 48
36	This Old Man	Pg 49
37	Three Blind Mice	Pg 50
38	Three Jolly Fisherman	Pg 51
39	Twinkle, Twinkle Little Star	Pg 52
40	Yankee Doodle	Pg 53

ACKNOWLEDGMENTS

Book two of the Porch Music Store Canjo music series features children's songs – not just for the young but also for the young at heart. As we discovered fun and easy to learn folk instruments on Holly's front porch, we drew a combination of new musicians from 3 to – well...double digit numbers. Most had never played an instrument before and the canjo became a favorite. Those days on the front porch inspired me to build simple folk instruments which then grew into the Porch Music Store and this Canjo book series.

Kathy Bartlett, who joined us on the front porch, researched, tested and compiled the songs in this book. She will likely caution you that musical instruments can become addictive. On that first front porch day, she owned one and now fills a room with dozens of folk instruments she is hoping her granddaughters learn to play as they grow.

The Gibbons Business Solutions team coordinated the project with Holly Gibbons and Kristie Haskins providing photography, Leigh Black graphic design, and Cheri Peace proofreading. Our child models, Audria, Cailynn, Lily and Sammie add their smiling faces.

Finally, we would like to acknowledge Herschal R. Brown of Jacksonville, NC, credited as having created the design of the canjo featured in this book. Brown freely shared his design with anyone who was interested in building canjos and is said to have made thousands of them for children everywhere – recouping his costs only. Mr. Brown loved the idea of making an instrument that anyone could learn to play and refused to copyright his canjo design. As a result, many builders are sharing his canjo vision in the US and beyond. And thousands more people are learning to play them.

Linda

How to Play the Canjo

The Canjo has a similar scale as the lap dulcimer or the Strum-stick. It's a diatonic scale: DO, RA, MI or **A, B, C, D, E, F, G** including the major notes of the music scale. It is the easiest of all instruments to play. You place your finger on the string just above the fret and each fret is a full note.

Music for the strum-stick, mountain dulcimer and Canjo are the same. Visit our website <u>www.porchmusicstore.com</u> for instructional videos. Follow the numbers; you'll be playing a song in minutes. To play with others, tune the open note to the key of the song.

You Are My Sunshine

0 3 4 5 5-
5 4 5 3 3-
3 4 5 6 8-
8 7 6 5- -
3 4 5 6 8-
8 7 6 5 3-
3 4 5- 6 4- 4 5 3- -

For example, if they are playing in the key of C – open string would be C. Key of D, open is D.

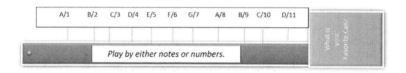

Play by either notes or numbers.

The diagram shows the neck layout and the numbers and notes on the fret board with tuning to open G. In other words, G is the note when you play the open string. (no finger on the fret) D-Tuning works great too! Remember there is only one string to keep in tune!

In this book, all songs are played by number.

Hold the canjo like a guitar or lay it on your lap. Strum at the bottom near the can. 0 is open string with no finger on a fret.

Place your finger on the string and move it up the neck. Just above every fret, there will be a full note. Follow the numbers in the song, and you will be playing a song in no time.

Below is a neck layout so you can see how the numbers and notes are placed on the fret board. This canjo is tuned to open G.

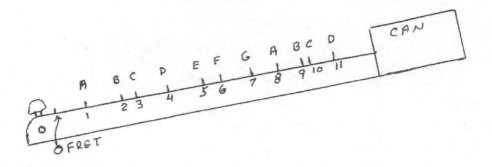

Canjo String Replacement

If your canjo string breaks it can be replaced with a guitar string. We recommend one of the higher strings, a B or high E, but any guitar string will work. We typically use a .013 gauge phosphor string.

First, remove the old string. Be sure to remove all the old wire from the tuning peg. This may require using a pair of needle nose pliers to pull the end as you unwind the string using the tuning peg.

Once you have removed all the old string, thread the new string into the hole at the bottom of the can. Pull the string toward the tuner. You will notice that the string is much longer than the canjo neck. Use nippers or wire cutters to shorten the string leaving about 4 inches excess.

Turn the tuning peg so you see the hole in the shaft. Thread the end of string into this hole. Then turn the tuning peg so the string threads over the top of the shaft. This step takes patience as you must push the string to insure it does not slip out of the hole until you get a turn or two wrapping the string around the tuning peg shaft. Keep turning until the string tightens up. There may be a pop as the string tightens and sets at the bottom of the can.

Tighten the string until you like the sound of the string played open. If you have a tuner, we typically tune to G or D. As mentioned previously, you can tune to whatever note you like. If you are playing with someone else, you will want to match what they are playing by tuning the open string to the key they are playing.

Let's Play!

Alouette

0	1	2	2	1	0	1	2	0	0
A	lou	et	te	gen	tille	A	lou	et	te

0	1	2	2	1	0	1	2	0
A	lou	et	te	je	te	plu	me	rai

0	1	2	3	4	4	4
Je	te	plu	me	rai	la	tete

4	5	4	3	2	1	0
Je	te	plu	me	rai	la	tete

4	4	4	0	0	0
Et	la	tete	Et	la	tete

4	4	4	0	0	0
A	lou	ette	A	lou	ette

4	3	2	1
A	lou	et	te

Alphabet Song

0	0	4	4	5	5	4
A	B	C	D	E	F	G

3	3	2	2	1	1	1	1	0
H	I	J	K	L	M	N	O	P

4	4	3	2		2	2	1
Q	R	S	*and*		T	U	V

4	4	3	3	2		2	1
W			X	Y	*and*		Z

0	0	4	4	5	5	4
Now	*I've*	*said*	*my*	*A*	*B*	*C's*

3	3	2	2	1	1	0
Tell	*me*	*what*	*you*	*think*	*of*	*me*

Baa Baa Black Sheep

0   0   4   4
Baa, baa, black sheep,
5   5   5 5   4
Have you any wool?
3   3   2 2
Yes sir, yes sir,
1   1   0
Three bags full.
4   4   4   3   3
One for my master,
2   2   2   1
One for my dame,
4   4   4   3   3   3
And one for the little boy
3   2   2   2   1
Who lives down the lane.
0   0   4   4
Baa, baa, black sheep,
5   5   5 5 4
Have you any wool?
3   3   2 2
Yes sir, yes sir,
1   1   0
Three bags full.

B-I-N-G-O!

0   3   3 3   0 1   1 0
There was a farmer had a dog,
0   3   3 4   4   5   3
And Bingo was his name-O.
5   5   6   6   6
B – I – N – G – O!
4   4   5   5   5
B – I – N – G – O!
3   3   4   4   4
B – I – N – G – O!
3   2   0 1   2 3   3
And Bingo was his name-O!

Buffalo Gals

0   0   0   2   4   4   5   4   4   2
Buf fa lo gals won't you come out to night

4   3   3   1   5   4   4   2
come out to night come out to night

0   0   0   2   4   4   5   4   4   2
Buf fa lo gals won't you come out to night

2 4   4   4   3   2   1   0
and dance by the light of the moon

CAMPTOWN RACES

4   4   4   2 4 5   4   2
The Camptown ladies sing this song,
2   1 2   1
Doo-da, Doo-da
4 4   4   2 4   5 4   2
The Camptown racetrack's five miles long
1   2 2   1 0
Oh, de doo-da day
0   0 2 4 7
Goin' to run all night
5   5 7   5   4
Goin' to run all day
4 4 4 2   2 4 4 5   4   2
I bet my money on a bob-tailed nag
1   2 3 2   1 1   0
Somebody   bet on the gray

Clementine

3 3 3 0   5 5 5 3
In a cavern, in a canyon
3 5 7 7 6 5 4
Excavating for a mine
4   5 6 6 5 4 5 3
Lived a miner, forty-niner
3   5   4   0   2   4   3
And his daughter, Clementine

3 3 3 0   5 5 5 3
Oh my darling, Oh my darling,
3 5 7 7 6 5 4
Oh my darling Clementine,
4   5 6   6   5   4 5 3
You are lost and gone forever,
3   5   4   0 2   4   3
Dreadful sorry Clementine.

Farmer in the Dell

0   3   3 3 3   3
The farmer in the dell

4   5   5 5 5   5
The farmer in the dell

7   7 8   7 5 3
Heigh ho the derry-o

4   5   5 4 4   3
The farmer in the dell

Frère Jacques

0   1   2   0   0   1   2   0
Frère Jacques, Frère Jacques,
2   3   4   2   3   4
Dormez-vous? Dormez-vous?
4   5   4   3   2   0   4   5   4   3   2   0
Sonnez les matines, sonnez les matines
0   1   0   0   1   0
Ding ding dong, ding ding dong.

0   1   2   0   0   1   2   0
Are you sleeping, are you sleeping?
2   3   4   2   3   4
Brother John, Brother John?
4   5   4   3   2   0
Morning bells are ringing,
4   5   4   3   2   0
morning bells are ringing
0   1   0   0   1   0
Ding ding dong, ding ding dong.

Go tell Aunt Rhody

5   5   4   3   3
Go tell Aunt Rhody,
4   4   6   5 4   3
Go tell Aunt Rhody,
7   7   6   5   3
Go tell Aunt Rhody
3   4   3   5   4   3
The old gray goose is dead.

HAPPY BIRTHDAY

0   0 1   0   3   2
Happy birthday to you
0   0 1   0   4   3
Happy birthday to you
0   0 7   5   3   2-1
Happy birthday dear (name)
6   6 5   3   4   3
Happy birthday to you

Home on the Range

0 0 3 4 5   3   2 1 6 6 6
Oh give me a home where the buf-fal-o roam,
5   6 7   3   3 3 2 3   4
Where the deer and the an-te-lope play,
0   0 3   4 5   3 2 1   6 6 6
Where sel-dom is heard a dis-cour-ag-ing word,
5   5 5   4   3 2   3 4 3
And the skies are not cloudy all day.

7   6   5 4 5
Home, home on the range,
0   0 3   3   3 3 2 3   4
Where the deer and the an-te-lope play,
0   0 3   4 5   3 2 1   6 6 6
Where sel-dom is heard a dis-cour-ag-ing word,
6   6 5   4   3 2   3 4 3
And the skies are not cloudy all day.

Hot Cross Buns

  2   1   0
Hot cross buns,
  2   1   0
Hot cross buns,
 0   0 0 0
One a penny,
1   1 1   1
Two a penny,
  2   1   0
Hot cross buns.

Hush, Little Baby

0   5 5 5 6   5   4   4 4
Hush, little baby, don't say a word.
0 0   4 4 4   4 5 4 3   3
Papa's gonna buy you a mockingbird

0 5   5   6 5   4   4
If that mockingbird won't sing,
0 0   4 4 4   4 5 4 3   3
Papa's gonna buy you a diamond ring

I Love You

4 2   4   4   2   4   5   4 3 2   1 2 3
I love you, you love me, We're a happy family
2   3 4   0   0   0   0 0   1   2   3 4
With a great big hug and a kiss from me to you.
3   1 1   3   2   1   0
Won't you say you love me too
4 2   4   4   2   4
I love you, you love me
5   4   3   2 1   2   3
We're best friends like friends should be
2   3 4   0   0   0   0 0   1   2   3 4
With a great big hug and a kiss from me to you.
3   1 1   3   2   1   0
Won't you say you love me too
4 2   4   4   2   4   5   4 3 2   1 2 3
I love you, you love me   We're a   happy family
2   3 4   0   0   0   0 0   1   2   3 4
With a great big hug and a kiss from me to you.
3   1 1   3   2   1   0
Won't you say you love me too

I'M A LITTLE TEAPOT

0   1 2 3 4   7
I'm a lit-tle teapot
5   7   4
Short and stout
3   3 4 2   2
Here is my handle
1   1 1   0
Here is my spout
0   1 2 3 4   7
When I get all steamed up
5 7 4
I just shout
7 5 4   3   2   1   0
Tip me over and pour me out

Itsy Bitsy Spider

0   0 0 0   1   2 2
The it-sy bit-sy spi-der
2   1 0 1 2 0
Climbed up the wa ter spout
2   2   3 4
Down came the rain
4   3   2 3   4 2
And washed the spi der out
0   0   1 2
Out came the sun
2   1   0 1 2 0
And dried up all the rain
0   0   0 0 1 2   2
And the it sy bit sy spi der
2   1 0 1   2 0
Climbed up the spout a gain

It's Raining, It's Pouring

3 3 1 4 3 1
It's raining, it's pouring;
3 3 1   4 3   1
The old man is snoring.
3 3   3 1 4
He went to bed and
3   3 1
bumped his head.
1 3   3 1 4 4 3 1
And couldn't get up in the morning.

Jesus Loves Me

4 2 2   1   2 4 4
Je-sus loves me! This I know,
5 5 7 5 5 4 4
For the Bi-ble tells me so;
4 2 2   1 2   4 4
Lit-tle ones to Him be-long;
5   5 4   0 2   1 0
They are weak, but He is strong.
4   2 4 5   7
Yes, Je-sus loves me!
4   2 0 2   1
Yes, Je-sus loves me!
4   2 4 5   7
Yes, Je-sus loves me!
5   4 0 2   1 0
The Bi-ble tells me so.

Kumbayah My Lord

0   2   4   4   5   5   4
Kumbayah my Lord, kumbayah
0   2   4   4   3   2   1
Kumbayah my Lord, kumbayah
0   2   4   4   5   5   4
Kumbayah my Lord, kumbayah
3   2   0   1   1   0
Oh Lord, kumbayah

London Bridge

4 5 4   3 2 3 4
Lon-don Bridge is fal-ling down,

1 2 3   2 3 4
Fal-ling down, fal-ling down,

4 5 4   3 2 3 4
Lon-don Bridge is fal-ling down,

1 4 2 0
My fair La-dy.

Mary Had a Little Lamb

2 1 0   1 2 2 2
Ma-ry had a lit-tle lamb
1 1 1   2 4 4
Lit-tle lamb, lit-tle lamb
2 1 0 1 2 2 2
Ma-ry had a lit-tle lamb
2 1   1 2   1 0
Its fleece was white as snow
2 1 0   1   2 2 2
Eve-ry-where that Ma-ry went
1 1 1   2   4 4
Ma-ry went, Ma-ry went
2   1 0   1   2 2 2
Eve-ry where that Ma-ry went
2 1   1 2   1 0
The lamb was sure to go
2 1   0 1 2   2   2
Fol-lowed her to school one day
1   1 1   2   4 4
School one day, school one day
2 1   0 1 2   2   2
Fol-lowed her to school one day
2   1   1 2 1 0
Which was against the rule

2   1 0 1 2   2 2
Made the child-ren laugh and play
1   1 1   2   4 4
Laugh and play, laugh and play
2   1 0 1 2   2 2
Made the child-ren laugh and play
2 1 1 2   1 0
To see a lamb at school

Oh Suzanna

0　1　2　　　4　　4　5　4　　　2
Oh I　come　from Al – a – bam – a
0　　1　　2　　　2　1　0　1
with my ban - jo on my knee,
0　1　2　　　4 4　　5　　4　　2
Oh I'm going to Lou – isi – an – a,
0　1　2　　2　　1　1　0
for my true love for to see.

3　　3　　　5　　5
Oh! Suz – an – na,
5　4　　4　2　0　1
Oh don't you cry for me,
0　1 2　　4　　4　5　4　　2
For I　come from Al – a – bam – a
0　　1　　2　　　2　1　1　0
with my ban – jo on my knee.

Old MacDonald Had a Farm

3   3   3   0 1   1 0
Old MacDonald had a farm
5   5   4   4   3
E – I – E – I – O
0   3   3   3   0 1   1 0
And on this farm he had a cow
5   5   4   4   3
E – I – E – I – O
0   0 3   3   3
With a moo moo here
0   0 3   3   3
And a moo moo there
3   3 3   3   3 3
Here a moo, there a moo
3   3 3   3 3 3   3
Everywhere a moo moo
3   3   3   0 1   1 0
Old MacDonald had a farm
5   5   4   4   3
E – I – E – I – O

ON TOP OF OLD SMOKEY

0   0   2 4 7   5
On top of Old Smo-key,
5 3   4 5   4
All cover ed with snow,
0 0   2   4   4   1
I lost my true lov er,
2   3   2   1   0
For court ing too slow.

ON TOP OF SPAGHETTI

0   0   2 4 7   5
On top of spa ghet ti
5 3   4 5   4
All cover ed with cheese
0 0   2   4   4   1
I lost my poor meat ball
2   3   2 1 0
When some bo dy sneezed

Pop Goes the Weasel

3 3   4 4   5 5   3
All around the cobbler's bench
0   3   3   4   6   5   3
The monkey chased the weasel,
0   3   3   4   4   5 5 3
The monkey thought 'twas all in fun
7   4   6   5   3
Pop! Goes the weasel.

Pussy Cat, Pussy Cat

2   1 0 2   1 0
Pussy cat, pussy cat,
4   4   4 4
Where have you been?
2   1   0 2 1   0
"I've been to London to
4 4 4 4
Vis-it the Queen."

0   1 2 0   1 2
Pussy cat, pussy cat,
3   3 3   5
What did you there?
5 4   2   0 4 2 0
"I frightened a little mouse
1   1 1   0
Under her chair."

Red River Valley

```
0    3   5  5  5  5   4   5  4   3
```
From that val ley they say you are leav ing,
```
0  3   5    3    5      7   6   5     4
```
we will miss your bright eyes and sweet smile.
```
7  6   5   5   4  3   4   5  7   6
```
For they say you are tak ing the sun shine
```
1   1   0   2     3   4    5 4 3
```
that sure brigh tens our path way a while.

Row, Row, Row Your Boat

0   0   0   1   2
Row, row, row your boat
2   1 2   3   4
Gent ly down the stream,
7   7 7 4   4 4 2   2 2 0   0 0
Mer-ri-ly, mer-ri-ly, mer-ri-ly, mer-ri-ly
4   3 2   1 0
Life is but a dream

Short'nin' Bread

7   5 5 4   4 7 7 5 4
Three lit-tle child-ren ly-in' in bed

7   5   4   3   3   2   2   1   0
Two was sick and the oth-er most dead

7   5 5   4   4   4   7   5 4
Sent for the doc-tor, the doc-tor said:

7   5   4   3   2   1   0
Feed those child-ren short-nin bread.

0   0   5 5 4 4 5   0   5   4   5
Mam-my's lit-tle ba-by loves short-nin, short-nin

7   7   5 5 4 4 3   2   1   0
Mam-my's lit-tle ba-by loves short-nin bread

Skip to My Lou

5   5 5   3   3   3
Fly's in the but ter milk,
5   5   7
Shoo, fly, shoo,
4   4 4   2   2   2
Fly's in the but ter milk,
4   4   6
Shoo, fly, shoo,
5   5 5   3   3   3
Fly's in the but ter milk,
5   5   7
Shoo, fly, shoo,
4   5 6   5   5   3   3
Skip to my Lou, my darlin'.
5   3   5   5   5   7
Lou, Lou, skip to my Lou,
4   2   4   4   4   6
Lou, Lou, skip to my Lou,
5   3   5   5   5   7
Lou, Lou, skip to my Lou,
4   5 6   5   4   3   3
Skip to my Lou, my darlin'.

Sleep My Child

3   2 1   3 4   3 2 0
Sleep my child, and peace att end thee
1 2   2 3
All through the night;
3   2 1 3 4 3 2   0
Guard ian an gels God will lend thee,
1 2   2 3
All through the night,

6 5 5   7 8   7 6   5
Soft the drow sy hours are creep ing,
6 5 4   3 5   4 3   2
Hill and vale in slum ber steep ing,
3 2 1 3 4 3 2   0
I my loving vigil keep ing,
1 2   2 3
All through the night.

Ten Little Indian

3   3 3 3   3 3
One little, two little,
5   7 7 5   3
Three little Indians.
4   4 4 4   4 4
Four little, five little,
2   4 4 2   0
Six little Indians.
3   3 3 3   3 3
Seven little, eight little,
5   7 7 5   3
Nine little Indians,
7   6 6 5   4 3   3
Ten little Indian boys.

This Old Man

4   2   4   4 2   4
This old man, he played one,
5   4   3   2
He played knick-knack
1   2   3
On my thumb.
4   4 4   0   0   0 0
With a knick-knack, paddy whack,
0   0   2   2 4
Give the dog a bone,
4   1   1   3   2 1   0
This old man came rolling home.

Two – Shoe
Three – Knee
Four – Door
Five – Hive
Six – Sticks
Seven – Up to heaven
Eight – On my gate
Nine – On my spine
Ten – Once again

Three Blind Mice

2   1   0   2   1   0
Three blind mice, three blind mice,
4   3   3   2   4   3   3   2
See how they run, see how they run,
4   7 7   6 5 6   7   4   4
They all ran after the farmer's wife,
4   7   7 7   6   5   6 7   4   4
Who cut off their tails with a carving knife,
4   7   7   6   5   6 7   4 4   4
Did you ever see such a thing in your life,
3   2   1   0
As three blind mice?

Three Jolly Fishermen

4   0   0   0 1 2   1 0
There were three jolly   fishermen
4   2   2   2 3 4 3 2
There were three jolly   fishermen
4 2 4 2 0   0   0
Fisher, fishermen, men, men
4 2 4 2 0   0   0
Fisher, fishermen, men, men
4   0   0   0 1 2   1 0
There were three jolly   fishermen

TWINKLE, TWINKLE LITTLE STAR

0   0   4   4   5 5 4
Twin kle, twin kle, lit tle star,
3   3 2   2 1   1   0
How I won der what you are.
4 4 3   3   2   2 1
Up a bove the world so high,
4   4 3 3   2 2   1
Like a dia mond in the sky.
0   0   4   4 5 5 4
Twin kle, twin kle, lit tle star,
3   3 2   2 1   1   0
How I won der what you are!

Yankee Doodle

3   3   4   5   3   5 4
Yan kee Doo dle went to town

3   3   4   5   3   2
ri ding on a   po ny

3   3   4   5   6 5   4
Stuck a fea ther in his hat

3   2   0 1   2   3   3
and called it   ma ca ro ni

ABOUT US

Porch Music Store is owned by Holly L. Gibbons and Linda Henderson.

We provide online resource for Folk Musicians providing quality products, information, lessons and workshops. We sell Ukuleles, Strum-sticks, Dulcimers, Mandolins, Guitars, Percussion Instruments, Tuners, Strings, Things and more…..

Ask us about our own handmade Canjos and CigarBox Ukuleles.

Interested in Booking a Workshop?
Learn how to build & play a Canjo
Learn how to play a Ukulele
History of Folk Music/Songs and more…

For more information about our products or workshops, contact porchmusicstore@gmail.com or call us at 814-657-6800.

We would love to hear from you.

Music is the language of the soul.

Made in the USA
Columbia, SC
30 November 2024